Earl of Abingdon

Thoughts on the Letter of Edmund Burke, esq., to the

Sheriffs of Bristol

on the affairs of America. Second Edition

Earl of Abingdon

Thoughts on the Letter of Edmund Burke, esq., to the Sheriffs of Bristol
on the affairs of America. Second Edition

ISBN/EAN: 9783337064693

Printed in Europe, USA, Canada, Australia, Japan

Cover: Foto ©ninafisch / pixelio.de

More available books at **www.hansebooks.com**

THOUGHTS

ON THE

LETTER of EDMUND BURKE, Esq;

TO THE

SHERIFFS of BRISTOL,

ON THE

AFFAIRS of AMERICA.

BY THE EARL OF ABINGDON.

THE SECOND EDITION.

O X F O R D,

Printed for W. Jackson: Sold by J. Almon, in Piccadilly, and J. Bew, in Paternoster-Row, London; and by the Booksellers of Bristol, Bath, and Cambridge.

[Price One Shilling.]

THOUGHTS

ON THE

LETTER OF EDMUND BURKE, Esq.

HAVING feen Mr. Burke's late Publication on the affairs of America, I was led to read it with all that attention which every performance of his muſt neceſſarily deſerve. I ſympathiſe moſt cordially with him in thoſe feelings of humanity, which mark, in language ſo expreſſive, the abhorrence of his nature to the effuſion of Human Blood. I agree with him in idea, that the War with America is "fruitleſs, hopeleſs, and unnatural"; and I will add, on the part of Great-Britain, cruel and unjuſt. I join hand in hand with him in all his propoſitions for Peace; and I look with longing eyes for the event. I participate with him in the happineſs of thoſe friendſhips and connexions, which are the ſubjects, ſo deſerved-

ly,

ly, of his panegyric. The name of Rocking-
ham is a facred depofit in my bofom. I have
found him difinterefted, I know him to be honeft. Before I quit him therefore, I will firft
abandon human nature.

So far then are Mr. Burke and I agreed. I
am forry that we fhould difagree in any thing.
But finding that we have differed, on a late occafion, in our Parliamentary Conduct; and that
I cannot concur with him in opinion on a matter, as I think, of very great national impor-
tance : it is therefore not in the zeal of party,
but in the fpirit of patriotifm, not to confute,
but to be convinced, not to point out error, but
to arrive at truth, that I now venture to fubmit
my thoughts to the Public. I feel the weight
of the undertaking, and I wifh it in abler hands.
I am not infenfible to my own incapacity, and
I know how much I ftand in need of excufe :
but as public good is my object, public candour,
I truft, will be my beft apologift.

Mr. Burke commences his Letter with the
mention of " the two laft Acts which have
" been paffed with regard to the Troubles in
" America." The firft is, " for the Letter of
" Marque," the fecond, " for a partial fufpen-
" fion of the *Habeas Corpus*." Of the former,
he

he ſays little, as not worthy of much notice. Of the latter, his diſtinctions are nice, his ſtrictures many, his objections unanſwerable; and yet, although ſo well appriſed of the dangers and miſchiefs of this Act, he ſays, " I have not " debated againſt this Bill in its progreſs through " the Houſe, becauſe it would have been vain " to oppoſe, and impoſſible to correct it." But this is matter of inquiry. As I thought differently, I acted differently. Being in the country, this Bill was in its way through the Houſe of Lords before I knew any thing of it. Upon my coming accidentally to town, and hearing of its malignity, I went down to the Houſe, I oppoſed it, and entered my ſolemn Proteſt on the Journals againſt it. It is true, I ſtood ſingle and alone in this buſineſs; but I do not therefore take ſhame to myſelf. Rectitude of intention will even ſanctify error. But Mr. Burke ſays, " During its progreſs through the Houſe " of Commons, it has been *amended,* ſo as to " expreſs more diſtinctly than at firſt it did, the " avowed ſentiments of thoſe who framed it." Now if the Bill was *amended* in its progreſs through the Houſe of Commons, Mr. Burke's reaſon " for not debating againſt the Bill" cannot be well founded; for his reaſon is, " that " it would have been vain to oppoſe, and *im-* " *poſſible to correct* it:" but to *amend* a thing is

to

to *correct* it ; and therefore if the Bill was *amended*, it was *not impoſſible to correct it.*

The caſe was this. This Bill was brought into the Houſe of Commons under the black coverture of deſigning malice. Some of the honourable Members of that Houſe, ſeeing it in this dark diſguiſe, endeavoured to unrobe it of its darkneſs. Their endeavours ſucceeded, and " it was *amended*, ſo as to expreſs more diſ-
" tinctly than it at firſt did, the avowed ſenti-
" ments of thoſe who framed it." In this ſhape it came to the Houſe of Lords : bad enough in all conſcience : but I uſe Mr. Burke's own words when I ſay, " there is a difference
" between bad and the worſt of all." I thought it bad, and therefore I put my negative upon it : had it been worſe, *a fortiori,* I ſhould have done the ſame. But here it would ſeem as if Mr. Burke and I were not agreed in our notions of *bad* and *worſe :* for what he holds *bad,* I eſteem *worſe,* and what he calls *worſe,* I think *bad.* To explain myſelf. He conſiders a *partial* Suſpenſion of the *Habeas Corpus* a greater evil than an *univerſal* ſuſpenſion of it. I conceive the contrary : though if Mr. Burke's premiſes were right, I ſhould approve his reaſoning, and admit his conſequences. He ſays " whenever
" an Act is made for a ceſſation of law and
" juſtice,

" juſtice, the whole people ſhould be univerſally
" ſubjeᴄted to the ſame ſuſpenſion of their
" franchiſes." Be it ſo: but then the whole
people ſhould fall under the reaſon and occaſion of the Aᴄt. If England was under the
ſame predicament with America, that is to ſay,
if Engliſhmen were looked upon to be Rebels,
as the Americans are, in ſuch a caſe, a *partial*
ſuſpenſion of the *Habeas Corpus* would be invi-
dious, and conſequently more unjuſt than a *general* ſuſpenſion of it; for why ſhould one Rebel
be diſtinguiſhed from another? but Engliſhmen are not accounted Rebels, and the Americans are; and therefore in the ſame degree that
a *partial* ſuſpenſion, on the one hand, *might* be
juſt, an *univerſal* ſuſpenſion, on the other,
would be unjuſt. Where the offence is local,
the puniſhment too muſt be local. It would
have been unjuſt if the lands in America had
been forfeited to the Crown in the year 1745,
becauſe Scotland was then in Rebellion. I do
not uſe theſe arguments in favour of the Bill.
The principle was *bad* with reſpeᴄt to America:
it was *worſe* with regard to this country. And
herein conſiſted the very malignity of the Bill:
for whilſt the *Habeas Corpus* was taken away
from the *imputed guilty* Americans, the *inno-
cent* Engliſh were at the ſame time deprived of
its benefit; ſuſpicion, without oath, being

A 4   made

made the two-edged fword that was to cut both ways.

But, fays Mr. Burke, "The alarm of fuch a "proceeding," (that is of an univerfal fufpenfion of the people's franchifes) "would then be "univerfal. It would operate as a fort of *call* "*of the nation.*" As to my part I have heard fo many *calls of the nation* of late, without any *anfwer* being made to them; that I fear the *nation* has either loft its *hearing* or its *voice:* but fuppofing otherwife, of what avail can a *call of the nation* be againft the fupremacy of an act of parliament? And who fhall dare to refift the authority of a ftatute that can alter the eftablifhed religion of the land, nay even bind *in all cafes whatfoever?* But more of this by and by.

Mr. Burke goes on to fay, "As things *now* "ftand, every man in the Weft-Indies, every one "inhabitant of three unoffending Provinces on "the Continent, every perfon coming from the "Eaft-Indies, every gentleman who has travelled "for his health or education, every mariner who "has navigated the feas, is, for no other offence, "under a temporary profcription." But how did things ftand *before the amendment* of the bill? Not only every man as defcribed above, but

every

every individual in this kingdom was under the
same temporary proscription. The writing of
a letter to, or receiving a letter from, America,
in this country, though the contents were ever
so harmless, was ground of suspicion sufficient
to immure a man in the castle of Dumfries, or
Pendennis, or wheresoever else persecution
should think fit to send him *. We have been
saved from this hell-governed proscription.
Opposition removed it from us. It had been
well to have done so from every subject of the
realm: but it did what it could, and the liberty of many unoffending persons has been
preserved thereby.

This being the state of the Bill, *amended*, as
Mr. Burke himself confesses, one might have
thought that, though *bad*, it was *better* than it
had been; but the very reverse of this is the
opinion of Mr. Burke : for in one place, he says,

---

* It is said that the number of persons who died in different
prisons during the despotic government of the Marquis de Pombal,
late minister of Portugal, *without having been convicted of any
crime*, is computed at 3970 persons ; and those who were lan-
guishing in irons at the time of his disgrace amounted to 800.
If this act had passed, as it was first framed, and if we may mea-
sure our punishments by those meted out to our brethren in America ; what reason is there to suppose that our situation had
not been the very counterpart of this ?

" the

" the limiting qualification, inftead of taking
" out the fting, does, in my humble opinion
" fharpen and envenom it to a greater degree."
And, in another, he adds, " that far from fof-
" tening the features of fuch a principle, and
" thereby removing any part of the popular
" odium or natural terrors attending it, I fhould
" be forry, that any thing framed in contradiction
" to the fpirit of our conftitution did not inftantly
" produce in fact, the groffeft of the evils, with
" which it was pregnant in its nature." So that
amendment, by foftening the features, and removing the popular odium, without producing
the groffeft of evils with which it was pregnant
in its nature, has, if I may ufe fuch terms of
contrariety, made the bill *worfe*. Such is the
doctrine of Mr. Burke, and juft it may be: but
if it be, I can only fay that he and I fee objects
through different mediums; and that if he
thinks it right to do evil that good may come
of it, I wifh to do good, by averting the evil.
The phyfician that ftops the progrefs of a
difeafe, may, at one time or another, hope for
its cure; but he that leaves the difeafe to the
efforts of nature alone, trufts to a caufe that is
very unfure in the effect. Mr. Burke, however,
in aid of his opinion fays, that, " On the next
" unconftitutional Act, all the fafhionable world
" will be ready to fay—Your prophecies are ri-
                                        " diculous,

" diculous, your fears are vain, you see how little
" of the mischiefs which you formerly foreboded
" are come to pass. Thus by degrees that artful
" softening of all arbitrary power, the alledged
" infrequency or narrow extent of its operation,
" will be received as a sort of aphorism: and Mr.
" Hume will not be singular in telling us, that
" the felicity of mankind is no more disturbed
" by it, than by earthquakes, or thunder, or the
" other more unusual accidents of nature." Now
as to the fashionable world, living as they do
under the tyranny of that greatest of all tyrants, *Fashion*, upon such an occasion, I should
hardly look up to them as a fit court of appeal.
And as to Mr. Hume, let those remember who
adopt his aphorisms—that that great philan-
thropist and friend of liberty, Doctor Franklin,
has not, in the depths of his wisdom thought,
" alledged infrequency or narrow extent of ope-
" ration," any argument to prevent the protection of mankind even " against the more un-
" usual accidents of nature;" and let them in
the remembring of this, regret, that his Politics, like his Philosophy, have not been the
subjects of our experiment. Happy, thrice
happy, had it been for this country, if, instead
of besetting this able man with foulmouthed
language, and indecent mockery, (indecent
doubly

doubly fo, becaufe of the venerable council before whom he ftood) his advice, like his *conductors*, had been made ufe of to draw the forked lightning from that portentous cloud, which, with overfpreading ruin, has now burft upon our heads.

Another argument made ufe of by Mr. Burke for not debating againft the Bill, is this. " It is," fays he, " fome time fince I have " been clearly convinced, that in the prefent " ftate of things, all oppofition to any meafures " propofed by minifters, where the name of " America appears, is vain and frivolous." I think fo too : but then, it does not therefore follow that oppofition is to be laid afide. The queftion, how far a member of either houfe can give over his attendance in Parliament, becaufe he is out-voted, is a nice queftion ; and worthy the examination of thofe who have leifure and abilities for the purpofe. My own private opinion is, that no member, *individually*, can do this, confiftently with his duty. *collectively* he may : as the precedent of feceffion, during the adminiftration of Sir Robert Walpole, fhews ; and as reafon proves : for it is not to be prefumed that a combination to this end can be obtained, without a fufficient foundation

foundation for it; and therefore when it does take place, it is intended, as Mr. Burke elsewhere fays, " as a fort of call of the nation." But even here, I muft not think it juftifiable, unlefs fupported on the following grounds. In the firft place, the feceffion muft be general; that is to fay, it muft not confift of this or that party only in oppofition, but muft include the whole Minority againft the meafures that have provoked feceffion. In the next place, it muft be a feceffion not *fub filentio*, but proclaimed either by Remonftrance on the Journals, or public Addrefs to the People; and when both thefe circumftances attend the act, then feceffion is not only juftifiable, but is the moft faithful pledge of duty that can be given. I have therefore exceedingly to lament that a feceffion, fuch as this is, has not been carried into execution; and not only on account of the proof that would have been given thereby to the nation of the fincerity of oppofition, but becaufe I do verily believe from my foul, that if it had, daring as Minifters are and have been, they would not have prefumed to have gone the lengths they have done in the open violation of the Conftitution; though upheld, as they fay they are, by Parliament, by the country gentlemen, and by their long tribe of obfequious addreffers.

But

But to return more directly, to the argument of Mr. Burke, and admitting that " all
" oppofition, where the name of America ap-
" pears, is vain and frivolous," and therefore
that Mr. Burke was right in not debating
againſt the Bill, the ſame reaſon muſt hold
good in every caſe of oppoſition where the
ſame circumſtances exiſt : for not to debate in
this inſtance, and to debate in another, " where
" the name of America appears," muſt be
wrong. Both cannot be right. And therefore Mr. Burke's repeated propoſitions ſo ably
made, and ſo well ſupported, for peace, might
have been diſpenſed with. Objections to taxes,
in aid of this deſtructive war, were unneceſſa-
ry. In ſhort all debate was

" Time miſpent, and language miſapplied:"

for " all oppoſition is vain and frivolous, where
" the name of America appears."

Having thus ſtated the reaſons, and examined
the motives that occaſioned *a difference in conduct* between Mr. Burke and me ; I ſhall now,
turning over thoſe many leaves of his letter, of
which, were I to take any notice, it muſt be in
admiration and in praiſe, proceed to that part
of it, wherein our *difference in opinion* prevails.
And here, in page 46, Mr. Burke ſays, " But I
" do

" do affure you, (and they who know me pub-
" lickly and privately will bear witnefs to me)
" that if ever one man lived, more zealous
" than another, for the fupremacy of Parlia-
" ment, and the rights of this Imperial Crown,
" it was myfelf." Now if I cannot join with
Mr. Burke in this folemn declaration of his, I
truft, it will not be therefore imputed to me,
that I am lefs zealous than he is for the rights
of the Britifh Legiflature; nor if I objeċt to the
terms of his propofition fhall I be condemned
as captious : for to cavil does not belong to me,
and more efpecially about words. But when I
fee, and know, and am perfuaded, that thefe
very modes of fpeech, *fupremacy of Parliament*,
rights of this imperial Crown, with their kindred
others, *unity of Empire*, *allegiance to the State*,
and fuch like high-founded *fefquipedalia verba*,
by becoming, in defiance of their impropriety,
the deities of modern invocation, and by ope-
rating as incantations to miflead mankind, have
done more mifchief to the State even than the
fword itfelf of Civil War; be their authority
ever fo great, I can never fubfcribe to their
ufe. *Supremacy of Parliament* is a combination
of terms unknown to the Englifh polity; and
as to *allegiance to the State*, though it be the
fanċtified phrafeology of an Archbifhop, it is,
like the " Whiggifm" he cenfures, allegiance
" run

" run mad." * Supremacy is an appendant of the Crown, and so is allegiance. The former is the right of the King, (as heretofore it was of the Pope) in his *ecclesiastical* capacity, the latter in his *temporal*; and there cannot be two rights, in one State, to the same thing. Who ever heard of the Oaths of Supremacy and of Allegiance to the Parliament? And why are they not taken to the Parliament? Because they are due to the King, and not to the Parliament; and it is not fit that the Parliament should invade " the rights of this Imperial Crown." Let each possess its own, and so the Constitution will be preserved. That the Parliament is *supreme*, I admit. It is the *supreme court*, or *curia magna* of the Constitution; as the House of Lords is the *supreme* court of Justice, or *dernier resort* of the Law. Both are *supreme*, and yet *supremacy* was never attributed to the House of Lords, but ever, in the language of the Constitution, belonged to the King, as the *supreme*

---

* Vide the Archbishop of York's Sermon, printed by T. Harrison and S. Brooke in Warwick-Lane, p. 22. It had been well if this, or any thing else that the Primate said, could have set aside the criminal charges to which his Sermon was exposed: but as it was indefensible, so is it matter of great national concern to .find such doctrines propagated by the once Tutor of the Heir-apparent to the Crown; though it prove of some consolation, as the Earl of Shelburne remarked, that his Majesty, perceiving the evil tendency of such principles, had, in his wisdom, removed him from the tuition of the Prince.

Head

Head of the Church. In like manner I admit, that the people are bound in obedience to the laws of Parliament : but this does not therefore infer " allegiance to the State." Allegiance is one thing, obedience another. Allegiance is due to the King, fo long as, in his *executive* capacity, he fhall protect the rights of the People. Obedience is due to the Laws, when founded on the Conftitution : but when they are *fubverfive* of the Conftitution, then difobedience inftead of obedience is due; and refiftance becomes the law of the land.

Thefe were my reflections, confequent on Mr. Burke's declaration; but my hope was, that although we differed in *words*, in *things* we might yet be agreed. How great then was my difappointment, when inftead of feeing this fubject unrobed of its gorgeous apparel, and like truth made to appear naked and unadorned, when inftead of difcuffion, which fuch a declaration feemed neceffarily to call for, when inftead of reafoning, and of argument, as if afraid of their confequences, I found affertions without the fhadow of proof, and precedents importing no authority, but upholding error, fubftituted in their room. " Many others, in-
" deed," fays Mr. Burke, " might be more
" knowing in the extent, or in the foundation

B   " of

" of thefe rights. I do not pretend to be an
" antiquary, or a lawyer, or qualified for the
" chair of profeffor in metaphyfics. I never
" ventured to put your folid interefts upon fpe-
" culative grounds. My having conftantly de-
" clined to do fo has been attributed to my in-
" capacity for fuch difquifitions; and I am in-
" clined to believe it is partly the caufe. I ne-
" ver fhall be afhamed to confefs, that where
" I am ignorant, I am diffident. I am indeed
" not very folicitous to clear myfelf of this im-
" puted incapacity; becaufe men, even lefs
" converfant than I am, in this kind of fub-
" tilties, and placed in ftations, to which I
" ought not to afpire, have, by the mere
" force of civil difcretion, often conducted the
" affairs of great nations with diftinguifhed
" felicity and glory." This may be very true,
but furely it is not very fatisfactory. To be
more zealous than any one man living " for the
" Supremacy of Parliament; and the Rights of
" this imperial Crown," and *lefs* knowing than
others " in the extent and foundation of thefe
" rights," is to profefs more of implicit faith
and enthufiafm, than, I confefs, I expected to
have met with, at leaft now adays, in *civil*
concerns. Of Fanatics in the Church I knew
there were ftill many to be found, but a State
Fanatic, I thought, was a *phænomenon* in politics

tics not of modern appearance. If indeed our Parliaments were, as our Scottish race of Kings held themselves to be, God's vicegerents, and governed the State *de jure divino;* then such a degree of belief had been only correspondent to the occasion of it: but Parliaments have ever been the works of men's hands, as, thank God, we now know that our Kings are; or otherwise we had not had our present most gracious Majesty on this throne, nor yet that additional solemn contract between King and People, I mean the *Act of Settlement*, for the eternal security, as I trust, of those Rights of the Subject which are intrusted to the executive power. Again, Why should a man be either antiquarian, lawyer, or metaphysician, or what need is there of speculation, to know " the extent " and foundation of these rights ?" The rights of Englishmen want no such professional authority for their support: neither are they mere abstract terms, the *entia rationis,* or creatures of the understanding; but are, for our knowledge, written in our hearts, with the blood of our ancestors. But " the affairs of great na- " tions are often conducted with distinguished " felicity and glory by the mere force of civil " discretion." What! are the rights of Englishmen to be held at the *discretion* of ministers?

nifters ? Is *civil difcretion* the rule of our government ? Wherein does *civil difcretion* differ
from *will*, the Law of Tyrants ?   And will any
minifter of this country fay, " I am not con-
" verfant in this kind of fubtilties, the extent and
" foundation of thefe rights," and therefore will
govern by this unconditional power, the mere
force of *civil d.fcretion?* This can never be :
but I have faid that I found affertions without
the fhadow of proof, and precedents importing
no authority, but upholding error; and this
obliges me to be more circumftantial.   The
fubject is a deep one ; and the confideration of
it the moft interefting of any that ever fell under political contemplation.   It is no lefs than
to know whether our *civil* exiftence has any
real foundation ; or whether, as it is faid of
the fea, it be without a bottom.   Perhaps
I may be loft in the depths of refearch : but if
I am, I carry this confolation with me, that I
fink in the caufe of truth.   I have this hope,
however, of prefervation about me, that I fhall
not dive into myfteries, nor yet venture among
the quickfands of metaphyfical abftractions.
The Conftitution of my country is the ground
on which I wifh to ftand, and if I gain this
fhore, my fafety prefent will reward the dangers paft.

Mr.

Mr. Burke having given us his Creed in the Supremacy of Parliament, next applies its *unlimited* power to and over the American Colonies ; and then tells us what the Supremacy of Parliament is in England. I fhall confider the laft firft, namely, the Supremacy of Parliament in England, as a major propofition in which the minor is contained. He fays (in order to fhew " the compleatnefs of the legiflative au-" thority of Parliament *over this kingdom*") that " if any thing can be fuppofed out of the power " of human legiflature, it is religion : I admit, " however, that the eftablifhed religion of this " country has been three or four times altered " by Act of Parliament; and therefore that a " Statute binds even in that cafe." This is con-clufive as to Mr. Burke's idea both with refpect to the *unlimited right* as well as the *unlimited power* of Parliament : but whilft he is fharp even to a point for the *general unlimited right* of Parliament, he adduces fome cafes to blunt the edge of its power *over this kingdom.* He fays, " But we may fafely affirm, that notwith-" ftanding this apparent omnipotence, it would " be *now* found as impoffible for King and Par-" liament to change the eftablifhed religion of " this country, as it was to King James alone, " when he attempted to make fuch an altera-" tion without a Parliament." Further : " I

" fee

" fee no abftract reafon, which can be given,
" why the fame power that made and repealed
" the High-Commiffion Court and the Star-
" Chamber might not revive them again : but
" the madnefs would be as unqueftionable as
" the competence * of that Parliament which
" fhould make fuch attempts." Furthermore :
" The King's Negative to Bills is one of the
" moft indifputed of the royal prerogatives, and
" it extends to all cafes whatfoever; but the ex-
" ercife is wifely foreborne." Moreover : " We
" know that the Convocation of the Clergy had
" formerly been called, and fat with nearly as
" much regularity to bufinefs as Parliament it-
" felf. It is now called for form only." Thefe
then are what I call precedents without authority, but upholding error : for diftinguifhing,
as muft be done, between *right* and *power*, Parliament cannot exercife a *power* without a *right*
to that *power* ; or if it does, it is an *ufurpation
of power*, which fooner or later never fails of redrefs. Precedents therefore of Acts of Parliament, repugnant to the fundamental principles
of the Conftitution, are no proofs of the Supremacy or Omnipotency of Parliament, but inftances only of the abufe of Parliament ; " and
" as no government," fays Machiavel, " can be

* It is prefumed that *incompetence* is here meant, and that *competence* is an error of the prefs.

" of

" of long duration, which, by the original
" formation of its conftitution, is not frequent-
" ly renewed or drawn back to its firft princi-
" ples," fo whenever this happens to us, as
it often has done, and, I truft, is again not afar
off from us, thefe precedents, like fo many
clouds difperfed, only ferve to fhew, that although they may darken the face of the conftitution, they can never extinguifh its light.

But a word or two more particularly of thefe
precedents. Much ftrefs has been laid on the
alterations that have been made in the eftablifhed religion, in order to fhew the right of Parliament to omnipotency: it is the doctrine of
Sir William Blackftone*: but as the moft able
chymift cannot extract *that* from any given
thing, *which* does not exift in its nature, fo is
this precedent, for this reafon, by no means a
cafe in point. In the firft place, religion has
nothing to do with the *civil* rights of the
State. It is fet apart from them, and belongs
to the Church ‡. The *civil* rights of the State
are of a *temporal* nature : they are *pofitive*, they

* Vide his Commentaries, vol. i. p. 161.
‡ I am aware how much I here differ from the very able Pre-
late, who is for harneffing Church and State together, like coach
and horfes, that He as one of the drivers may enjoy the fmack
of the whip; a fmack which he cannot forget, and which he
gave me reafon to remember when I was at Weftminfter fchool :

but

are *general,* affecting every member of the
community equally and alike. Religion is of
a *spiritual* nature: it is a *negative* duty, and
not a *positive* right: it is *not general,* but varies
according to men's consciences: it is the fubject of *toleration,* for no laws can have power
over men's minds. What Act of Parliament
can make me believe that *three* is *one,* or *one* is
three, if I do not chufe to believe it? Or that
my falvation in the next world is to be obtained
by the belief of 39 Articles in this? The *efta-*
blifhed religion, therefore, is no more than that
drefs which the *State taylors* have provided for
Religion to go to *court* in; and the fame *taylors*
that made this *drefs,* can *alter* it, as we have
feen, and as the fafhion of the times changes.

But if this was not the cafe with the eftablifhed religion, how, in the next place, does
its alteration fhew the right of Parliament to
omnipotency? What effect has it had on the
conftitution? Are we *lefs* free now, either in
Church or State, than we were before the Re-
formation? I fhould imagine that we are *more*
free in both, and if fo, freedom being the firft
principle of the conftitution, the *power* of Par-

but as I am now out of his clutches, fo I hope I am out of his
books too, at leaft fuch as are akin to his political fermons.
Vide Archbifhop of York's Sermon, p. 10.

liament

liament to alter the *eſtabliſhed* religion has been
but correſpondent to its *right*; and therefore,
whilſt it is no proof of the ſupremacy of Parliament, I ſhould not be ſorry to ſee a little
more alteration of it.   I think it may ſtill be
amended, without offence to the people, or in-
jury to the conſtitution; nay even with ſatis-
faction to ſome of the clergy themſelves.   The
ſecond precedent is that of the High Commiſ-
ſion Court, and the Star Chamber; which is
in direct proof of my argument :   for they,
being uſurpations of *power*, and abuſes of the
right of Parliament, have been diſſolved; and
therefore I agree with Mr. Burke that it would
be madneſs to revive them, and for the reaſon
he gives too, to wit, " the incompetence of
" Parliament :" though if the power of Parliament be *unlimited*, is not the *incompetency* of
Parliament a poſition ſomewhat paradoxical ?
The third precedent is, " the King's negative
" to Bills, which is wiſely forborne."   This is
the forbearance of a *known right* to a *power*
veſted by the conſtitution in the Crown, and
not the exerciſe of a power *unknown* to the
conſtitution.   As it therefore ſhews, that, even
where there is a manifeſt *power*, that *power* is
limited ; ſo it proves, of courſe, that where
there is no manifeſt *power*, there can be no
right to *unlimited power*.   The laſt precedent
is

is that concerning the Convocation of the Clergy; and to this, what I have faid on the head of the *eftablifhed* religion, inafmuch as *ecclefiaftical* matters have nothing to do with *civil* concerns, may here be applied. But I do not recollect that, in bringing the Convocation of the Clergy to its prefent *formal* ftate only, there was any exertion of power of any kind to this end. If I remember aright it was a bargain. It was agreed that, on their Convocations becoming merely paffive, the beneficed Clergy fhould pay no further fubfidies to the government, as they ufed to do in Convocation; and that they fhould be *reprefented* in Parliament, by being allowed to vote at the elections for Knights of the Shire : for before this they were not *reprefented* in Parliament, but in their own Convocations; and therefore Parliament had no *right* to tax them, nor were they taxed by Parliament, notwithftanding its *unlimited power*, and " the compleatnefs of its legiflative " authority over this kingdom."

If this then be the refult of thefe precedents, and the State of what has been offered by Mr. Burke *for* this *arbitrary right* in Parliament, extending even to Religion itfelf, and whofe *power* is limited *only* by " the mere force of " civil difcretion;" is there nothing further that

may

may be faid *againſt* this *right ?* I ſhall conſider.
There is nothing ſo much talked of, and yet
nothing ſo little underſtood, as the *Engliſh Conſtitution.* Every man quotes it, and upon every
occaſion too : but few know where to find it.
If one enquire after it, an Act of Parliament is
produced. If you aſk what it is, you are told
it is the *Law.* Strange miſtake ! The *Conſtitution* and the *Law* are not the ſame. They differ and in what manner I will endeavour to
point out. In the great *machine* of State there
are found three *principal powers,* with a variety
of others ſubordinate to them ; particularly the
Prerogative of the Crown : which is a *power*
there veſted not to counteract the *higher powers,*
but, if at any time there ſhould be occaſion, to
ſupply their deficiencies. The firſt of theſe
principal Powers, is the *Power* of the *People ;*
the ſecond, the *Power* of the *Conſtitution ;* the
third, the *Power* of the *Law.* Now the *Power*
of the *People* is firſt, becauſe, without People,
there could be neither *Conſtitution* nor *Law.*
The *Power* of the *Conſtitution* is ſecond, for it
is the immediate effect of this firſt cauſe ; and
if the *People* and the *Conſtitution* make the firſt
and the ſecond *Power,* there is no need to prove
that the *Law* is the third *Power* of the State.
It follows in the order I have laid down.
As from the *People* then is derived the *Conſtitu-*
tion,

tion, ſo from the *Conſtitution* is derived the *Law*; the *Conſtitution* and the *Law* being, in a due courſe of lineal conſanguinity, the deſcendants of the *People*.

But now I ſhall be aſked, what is this *Conſtitution,* and what is this *Law?* I anſwer, that by pointing out their relations, their differences too are marked. But this is not enough : definition is neceſſary, and therefore, as a definition *of the name* I would ſay, that *Conſtitution* ſignified *Compaƈt,* and was the ſame with *public or political Law*; and that *Law,* as here meant, was the *municipal or civil Law* of the State : but as a definition *of the thing,* perhaps *both* may beſt appear as derived the one from the other. I define *Conſtitution* then to be, thoſe *Agreements* entered into, thoſe *Rights* determined upon, and thoſe *Forms* preſcribed, by and between the Members of any Society in the firſt ſettlement of their union, and in the frame and mode of their Government; and is the *Genus* whereof the *municipal or civil Law* of ſuch eſtabliſhed Community is the *Species:* the *former,* aſcertaining the reciprocal duties, or ſeveral relations ſubſiſting betwixt the *governors and governed*; the *latter,* maintaining the rights and adjuſting the differences ariſing betwixt individuals, as parts of the ſame whole. And this I take

take to be the true diftinction, and real difference between the *Conftitution* and the *Law* of
England. But this is matter of *Theory* only. It
is the *paffive* ftate of Government, and Government muft be *active*. *Practice* therefore is to be
fuperadded to this *Theory*; and hence the origin of *Parliaments*. What then are *Parliaments?* *Parliaments* make the *formal*, as *Rights*
do the *fubftantial*, part of the Conftitution;
and are the Deputies, the Agents, or Appointees
of the People, entrufted by them with the
Powers of *Legiflation*, for the purpofe of pre-
ferving (and not of deftroying) the eftablifhed
Rights of the Conftitution. But what are the
eftablifhed Rights of the Conftitution? In detail,
they are multifarious, and many : but reduced
to their firft principles, they are thefe, "*Security*
" *of Life, Liberty, Property, and Freedom in*
" *Trade.*" Such are the great Outlines of the
Englifh Conftitution, the fhort hiftory, or abftract
of that *original Compact*, which is the bond or
cement of our civil union, and which forms, in
particular, the relations that exift betwixt the
legiflative Power of the State, and the *People*.
But there is ftill another relation to be confidered.
The *legiflative Power* of the State muft receive
its force from an *executive Power*. This *executive Power* is lodged in the *Crown*, from
whence a relation arifes betwixt the *Crown* and
People; and is called " the Contract between
" King

" King and People." As *Compact* then is that
Agreement of the People with the *legiſlative
Power*, or among themſelves, concerning their
ſame Rights ; ſo *Contract* is that *Bargain* of the
People with the *executive Power* concerning
their *different* Rights *. But here it will be

---

* Writers upon this ſubject have confounded the two terms,
Compact and *Contract* together; making them to ſignify one
and the ſame thing, though *really* different. *Compact* is an
Agreement entered into without any other conſideration, than
that of the plighted faith of the parties to the articles agreed
upon : for the articles being *general*, it is equally the intereſt of
every *individual* to obſerve them without any additional obliga-
tion ; and ſuch is the *original Compact*, or *Conſtitution* of this
country. But *Contract* is a *Bargain*, with a *condition* annexed
thereto, that demands a *quid pro quo* ; and ſuch is the " Con-
" tract between King and People": for the *executive Power* being
lodged in the *Crown*, the *King* may ſuffer the Laws to ſleep, or
pervert them " from their right uſe to their worſt abuſe," which,
making the articles of this Contract *not general*, calls for different
covenants ; and therefore the King, at his coronation, takes an
oath to protect the Rights of the People ; and the People, in return, owe, and may be called upon to ſwear, Allegiance to the
King. It may be further obſerved, that as it was not to be ſup-
poſed that Parliaments, whoſe rights were preciſely the ſame
with thoſe of the People, could poſſibly enact Laws ſubverſive of
thoſe Rights, ſo the *original Compact* ſeeming to require no other
ſanction, no other agreement between the legiſlative Power and
the People was ever thought of : but now Corruption, that ſelf-
devouring monſter of the State, making freſh covenants neceſſary, it is to be hoped, that the ſame *explicit, unevaſive, expreſs*
Contract, which exiſts between the King and People, will ſoon,
very ſoon, be made to ſubſiſt between the Parliament and People.
It was the doctrine of *unlimited Power* in the Crown that obtained
the former ; it is the now new and more dangerous doctrine of
unlimited Power in Parliament that muſt procure the latter.

ſaid,

faid, How is this known, and where is this to be found? I reply, As well in the reafon of the things themfelves, and our own experience, as in the letter and fpirit of our Charters: for inftance, in *Magna Charta*, which is not only declaratory of the *original Compact*, or fundamental Rights of the People, but is *itfelf* that *folemn Contract*, which was had between King and People, for the protection of thofe Rights; and therefore, as fuch, proves *quod erat demonftrandum*.

But now I may be told, that although I have made a diftinction between the *Conftitution* and the *Law* of England, I have cited *Magna Charta*, which is an Act of Parliament, and confequently the Law of England, as for the *Conftitution* of England. The objection is fpecious only, for it is groundlefs. In the firft place, it is not true that *Magna Charta* is an Act of Parliament; and for this reafon: that it was obtained in the field of battle, with fword in hand, in Runing-Mead, between Windfor and Staines, where the *People* had pitched their tents, and where, as hiftory further informs us, " King John and his adherents ap-" peared to be an inconfiderable number, but " the Lords and Commons filled the country."

It

It is therefore true, that *Magna Charta* was the Act of the People *at large*, and not of the Legiflature *alone*. Befides: it is proved by Acts of Parliament, that it is not an Act of Parliament; and that Parliament (*unlimited* as its power is now faid to be) has no power over it at all: for it is declared by the ftatute of the 25th of Edw. I. that *Magna Charta* was obtained by the *common Affent of all the Realm*, and that it was to be received as the *Folcright*, or common Law of the Land. And by the 43d of Edw. III. all ftatutes made againft *Magna Charta* are declared to be void: fo that whilft *Magna Charta* proves the *Conftitution* to be anterior to the Law, Acts of Parliament fhew that it is not fubject to the Law, nor under the power of Parliament. But, in the next place, admitting *Magna Charta* to be an Act of Parliament, ftill the objection remains without foundation. For *Magna Charta*, being not *enactive* of new Rights, but, as I have faid before, *declaratory* only of thofe old Rights of the People, fome of which are of Saxon anceftry, others coeval with the firft form of Britifh Government, is a Law only in proof of the Conftitution; and therefore fupports my pofition, that the *Conftitution* and the *Law* are not the fame.

But

But there is still another objection, which I must anticipate in order to remove. It may be objected, that if (as I have shewn) *the People be made the source of all power in the State*, in what manner is such an idea to be reconciled with the doctrine, that " Government certainly " is an Institution of divine Authority ?" * for these (upon another occasion) are the words of Mr. Burke; though, he adds, that its *Forms* and the *Persons* who administer it, all originate from the People. What a pity that an " In- " stitution of divine Authority" should ever be found in the hands of *Devils*, as our Government sometimes unhappily is! But I do not mean to enter into the merits of this doctrine. Indeed I am bound not to do so: for I have said, that I will not dive into mysteries, lest I be drowned; and I will keep my word. But as this said mode of attributing to *natural* effects *supernatural* causes, or mixing Church and State together, has already done a great deal of mischief to the community; as I perceive that the *divine Right* of Parliaments, like the *divine Right* of Kings, to do what is *wrong*, with its concomitant train, *passive obedience* and *non-resistence*, is now from the

" Pulpit, drum ecclesiastic,
" That's beat with fist, instead of a stick,"

* Vid. Thoughts on the Cause of the present Discontents, fifth edit. p. 67.

C   founding

founding forth in the ears of the * People ; as
I am content to judge of things *paft* by the
prefent, leaving to others all better rules of
judging ; and inafmuch as example goes before
precept ; fo the prefent ftate of America afford-
ing not only much notable information on this
head, but ferving to illuftrate the whole of
what has been here faid on the fubject of Go-

---

* See a Sermon preached before the Univerfity of Oxford, on
Friday; December 13, 1776, being the day appointed by pro-
clamation for a general Faft. By Myles Cooper, LL. D. Pre-
fident of King's College, New-York, and Fellow of Queen's
College, Oxford. Publifhed at the requeft of the Vice-Chan-
cellor and Heads of Houfes, and printed at the Clarendon prefs.
This Doctor fays, p. 12. " It is difficult indeed to affign any
" reafons that will juftify the Rebellion of Subjects againft the
" fovereign Authority." " Submiffion to the higher Powers"
" is enjoined at leaft upon Chriftians, under the fevereft penalty.
" But were Chriftianity altogether out of the queftion, yet the
" infurrection of fubjects againft their rightful Governors, is
" condemned by thofe Laws which are fundamental to fociety."
He fays too, p. 22. " When men's principles are wrong, their
" practices will feldom be right. When they fuppofe thofe
" Powers to be derived folely from the People, which are or-
" dained of God, and their heads are filled with ideas of ori-
" ginal Compacts *which never exifted*, and which are always
" explained fo as to anfwer their prefent occafions ; no wonder
" that they confound the duties of rulers and fubjects, and are
" perpetually prompted to dictate where it is their bufinefs to
" obey. When once they conceive the *governed* to be fuperior
" to the *governers*, and that they may fet up their *pretended*
" *natural Rights* in oppofition to the *pofitive Laws* of the State ;
" they will naturally proceed to " defpife dominion and fpeak
" evil of dignities," and to open a door for anarchy, confufion,
" and every evil work, to enter." What *more* did Sacheverel
fay ? And yet Sacheverel was impeached, whilft Doctor Cooper
may expect preferment.

vernment,

vernment, I shall, with some advantage I trust, and in as few words as I can, make use of the instance.

America, having declared itself independent of Great-Britain, returned to that state of Nature, or state of Society, where Government was to be instituted; and being so circumstanced, whilst it proceeded to form itself into separate Commonwealths, or States, each Commonwealth or State provided a Constitution or Form of Government of its own; which, although differing in mode and manner, agreed in substance and effect. The Precedent therefore of one Constitution answering for every other, I shall here avail myself of such extracts from the Constitution of *the State of Massachusetts*, as are necessary to my purpose. This Constitution then, or Form of civil Government, consists of forty-three Articles, and is entitled, " An Act of the *General Convention* of " the Commonwealth, or State of Massachusetts, " declaring the same to be a free State, and " independent of Great-Britain, and establish- " ing a new Constitution and Form of civil " Government; which *General* Convention " was elected by *the whole People* for this *sole* " *purpose*, &c." It next recites those (but too much to be lamented) arbitrary and despotic measures of this country, which occasioned the

C 2 Declaration

Declaration of Independency; and after this,
proceeds to fay, " The antient Government
" of this Colony being thus *totally diffolved,*
" and the People driven into *a State of Nature,*
" it becomes their indifpenfible duty, and what
" felf-prefervation requires, to declare them-
" felves independent of Great-Britain, and to
" eftablifh fuch a Conftitution and Form of
" civil Government, as to them appears beft
" calculated to promote their greateft poffible
" happinefs:" " And whereas it is abfolutely
" neceffary for the welfare and fafety of the
" inhabitants of this Commonwealth, that a
" juft and permanent Conftitution and Form of
" civil Government fhould be eftablifhed as
" foon as poffible, *derived from and founded on*
" *the authority of the People only, in whom is*
" *the origin of all governmental Power,* and
" who have at all times a right, by *common*
" *confent* (whenever the great end of Govern-
" ment, the general good is not obtained) to
" alter and change their Conftitution and Form
" of Government, in fuch manner as may beft
" promote the fafety and happinefs of the
" whole."

" We, therefore, the Reprefentatives of the
" Freemen of Maffachufetts, in *general Con-*
" *vention* met, for the *exprefs purpofe* of fram-
" ing fuch a Conftitution and Form of Go-
" vernment,

" vernment; gratefully acknowledging the
" goodnefs of the fupreme Governor of all, in
" permitting us peaceably, and *by common con-*
" *fent*, deliberately to form fuch rules, as we
" fhall judge beft adapted for governing this
" Commonwealth in juftice and righteoufnefs;
" and being fully convinced that it is our in-
" difpenfible duty to eftablifh, to the utmoft
" of our power, fuch *original principles* of civil
" Government, as will beft promote the gene-
" ral happinefs of the People, do, by virtue of
" the authority vefted in us by our Conftituents,
" declare, enact, and eftablifh the following
" Conftitution, and Form of civil Government,
" for this Commonwealth, to be and remain
" in full force therein, from and after the fe-
" cond Wednefday in ————, and *forever*
" *thereafter to remain unaltered*, except in fuch
" articles as fhall hereafter, on new circum-
" ftances arifing, or on experience, be found
" to require alteration; and which fhall, *by the*
" *like authority of the People, convened for that*
" *fole purpofe*, be altered, for the more effectual
" obtaining and fecuring the great end and
" defign of all good Government, *the Good of*
" *the People.*"

" Be it therefore declared and enacted by
" the *general Convention* of this Common-
" wealth, affembled *for the fole purpofe* of de-

" claring

" claring and enacting Independency, and efta-
" blifhing a new Conftitution and Form of
" civil Government, and by the authority of
" the fame, it is hereby declared and enacted,
" as in the following general articles, viz.

1. " That this Colony is, and of right ought
" to be, and for ever hereafter fhall, by the
" favour of all-gracious Heaven, be a free
" State, and abfolutely independent of the
" Crown and Government of Great-Britain;
" and fhall be ftyled, THE COMMONWEALTH,
" OR STATE OF MASSACHUSETTS."

5. " That this declaration of the general,
" fundamental, and effential Rights of the
" People of this Commonwealth, fhall, *for*
" *ever hereafter*, be confidered as the general
" fundamental of the faid new Conftitution
" and Form of Government; *and every order,*
" *law, and ftatute, that fhall hereafter be made*
" *by the general Court of this Commonwealth,*
" *fhall conform to the fpirit, and plain fimple*
" *meaning and intention of thefe general funda-*
" *mentals; and all and every order, law, and*
" *ftatute, that may hereafter happen to be made,*
" *and fhall be found contrary thereto, fhall be*
" *null and void, and have no effect, and be im-*
" *mediately repealed: and no alteration in thefe*
" *general fundamentals fhall hereafter be made,*
" *but only by the immediate confent of the good*
" *People*

" *People of this Commonwealth at large, or their*
" *deputies, chosen for that special purpose.*"

6. " That all men are born equally free
" and independent, and *their Maker has left*
" *them free liberty to set up such Governments as*
" *best please themselves.*" " That Magistrates
" were set up for the good of Nations, not
" Nations for the honour and glory of Magi-
" strates." " That the Right and Power of
" Magistrates in every country, was that which
" the Laws of that country made it to be."
And, " That usurpation gives no right to
" govern."

7. " That all men have a natural and un-
" alienable right to worship God according to
" the dictates of their own consciences, and
" to enjoy a full and free liberty therein ; pro-
" vided that they, under pretence of Religion,
" do not attempt to subvert the Constitution
" and Form of Government of this State, &c."

Here then is that in *esse,* what Dr. Cooper
tells us " never existed," *an original Compact.*
A Compact too, with *Powers* (which, according to him, " are ordained of God") *solely* derived from the People ; and, the *governed* being superior to the *governors,* with natural
Rights, " pretended," as he says they are, " set
" up in opposition to the positive Law of the
" State."

" State." Such is this Compact, and such, I presume, being all other *original* Compacts in their firft inftitution, it is no wonder that their exiftence fhould be denied; inafmuch as they are the fovereign antidotes of thofe political poifons, *Prieſt-Craft*, and *State-Craft*, whofe objects are dominion over " the Beafts of the " People*."

Here too is an " inftitution of Government," but where " the divine authority" of it is, who can difcover? Indeed, in a century more, for we are already giving up *things* for *words*, *senfe* for *found*, and from the *golden* falling back into the *iron* age again, fuch notions of Government may be well received. Tradition will inform pofterity that the Governments of America were inftituted *de Jure divino*, and not without fome reafon on their fide; inafmuch as the more *natural* any Government is, in my opinion the more *divine* it is: but now that we

---

* Such is Doctor Cooper's *humane* appellation of thofe perfons in America, who plundered, as he fays, the Members of the Church of England, Him, I fuppofe, among the reft, and others, of their property; adding, " without any means of pre" fent redrefs, though it is to be hoped, not without a profpect " of future retribution." Methinks the Doctor, having received a flap on one cheek, in the true fpirit of a Chriftian, fhould have turned the other, and not have looked forward to a profpect of plundering the Americans of their property, becaufe they had plundered him of his. However, whenever the Americans fhall come to this country to deprive us of *our Liberties*, I will readily join the Doctor in his idea of Retribution.

are

are witnesses to their *inflitution*, we know, we see, and we find that they are inflituted *de Jure humano*.

The next obfervation to be made is the affinity of thefe Governments to that of our own country. They are founded on original Compact, and fo is ours. The lines of diftinction betwixt the People, the Conftitution, and the Law, are marked there as they are drawn here. The Conftitution is derived from the People, and the Law from the Conftitution. The Law cannot alter the Conftitution : for all and every Law and Statute that are, by the *general Courts*, (equal to our Parliaments) made contrary thereto, are null and void : neither is the Conftitution *alterable*, but by general Conventions of the People *at large*, held *exprefsly* and *folely* for that purpofe.

If now then I fhould profefs to believe that there is no more of *divine authority* in the Government of England, than in the Governments of America, a fample of which has been produced ; and that the former is derived from the fame powers, by the fame means, and to the fame end, namely, the *good of the whole*, as the latter : I hope I fhall not be therefore accounted an *Infidel* by the *Church*, nor an *unworthy Member of Society* by the *State*. I muft hope too, that if our *Parliaments*, who are the

Truftees

Truftees of the People, and the *Guardians* of their rights, (for they are no more, and I am one of its Members) fhould ever attempt to deftroy thofe rights, that, as they will well deferve the fate, fo may they feel all that vengeance which the offended *Majefty* of an injured People can bring down on their heads. Parliaments who will fupport the Conftitution, will be fupported by the People, and have nothing to fear; but thofe who will fubvert the Conftitution, let them tremble, as one man, even as Charles the Firft did, who loft his head in fuch an attempt; and which, as Lord Chefterfield tells us, " if he had not loft, we had certainly " loft our Liberties."

Having thus gone over the conftitutional ground of this country, and taken a comparative view of the foundation upon which its Government is fuperftructed, the inference to be drawn from thence is this; that if the Government be as I have ftated it to be, and as I fhall hold it to be, till the contrary be proved, the *right to unlimited power* contended for in Parliament, cannot, in common apprehenfion, there exift. For although Mr. Burke afferts (and I mention this, becaufe I wifh to ftate, and not to miftate his meaning, and if I do, I truft he will impute it to the want of comprehenfion, and not to any intention in me)

" that

" that Legiſlators ought to do what Lawyers
" cannot; for they have *no other* rules to bind
" them but the great principles of reaſon and
" equity, and the general ſenſe of mankind;"
and although in arbitrary countries this is true,
for there the People being *diveſted* of all power,
and both the legiſlative and executive authority
veſted ſolely in the Prince, he may have no
other rules than theſe to bind *him*; yet in free
countries the caſe is different. In England,
" the legiſlative," ſays Lord Bolingbroke, " is
" a *ſupreme*, and may be called, in one ſenſe,
" an *abſolute*, but in none an *arbitrary* power."
" It is *limited*," ſays Mr. Locke, " to the pub-
" lic good of the Society." I ſay, it is bound
by the rules of the Conſtitution, for the rules
of the Conſtitution are to the Parliament, what
the Law is to the Judges. The People make the
Conſtitution, the Parliaments make the Law;
and as the Judges are bound to determine according to the Law of the land, ſo are Parliaments bound to enact Laws according to the
rules of the Conſtitution; and not according to
their own principles of reaſon and equity, and
what they call the general ſenſe of mankind:
for theſe *may* differ with the principles of the
Conſtitution, as we know they *have* done; and
therefore ariſes the neceſſity of aſſerting the
controul of the Conſtitution over the Law and
the Parliament.

But

But of this power of the Conftitution over the legiflative authority Mr. Burke has himfelf given the moft pointed cafe. He fays, " before " this Act (that is before the Act for the partial " fufpenfion of the Habeas Corpus) every man " putting his foot on Englifh ground, every " ftranger owing only a local and temporary " allegiance, even a Negro flave, who had been " fold in the Colonies, *and under an Act of* " *Parliament*, became as free as every other ": man who breathed the fame air with him." What is it then that, fetting this Act of Parliament at defiance, manumits the Negro-flave fo foon as he puts his foot on Englifh ground'? Let it not be faid that it is *the pure air* of this foggy ifland, that can work thefe wonderful wonders, for thefe are the half-witted fayings of lawyers that would be orators, and fit only for the *lullabies* of nurfes, or the *fingfongs* of children. Let it not be faid that the Act is local; for it is not local. The Act alluded to is the 5th of G. II. ch. 27. (but there are many other Acts to the fame effect) and it vefts a clear and unconditional property, confined no where, but abfolute every where, in the owner to his purchafed flave; and yet when this owner fhall bring his flave to this country, he fhall lofe his ownerfhip in him; though he hold him under an Act of Parliament. No: it is neither the one, nor the other, that gives

occafion

occasion to this manumission. It is the Constitution of England, which maintaining *liberty*,
and annihilating *slavery*, renders this Act of
Parliament a *tabula rasa*, a blank parchment,
without operation, without force, without effect.
*It is that Constitution, which is now resisting the
rebellion of Acts of Parliament against it.* In
short, my idea of this Government, to speak as a
lawyer would do, is, that *Parliaments*, as I have
said before, are the trustees of the People, the
Constitution the deed of trust, wherein they
stand seized to *uses* only; and these *uses* being
named, they cannot depart from them : but for
their due performance are accountable to those
by whose conveyance the trust was made.
The *right* is therefore *fiduciary*, the *power limited*. Or as a mathematician would say,
more in the road of demonstration; the *Constitution* is a *Circle*, the *Laws* the *Radii* of that
Circle, drawn on its surface with the pen of
Parliament, and it is the known quality of a
circle, that its *radii* cannot exceed its *circumfe-
rence*, whilst the People, like the *compasses*, are
fixed in the center, and describe the *circle*.
These, I say, are my ideas of this Government,
that is, of the whole political system of this
country, for this is what I would mean by
Government, and I hope that they are just
and true; or otherwise, dreadful indeed is the
prospect before us! For if Parliaments have
the right to alter the " established religion of
the

" the land," and " if any thing can be fup-
" pofed out of the power of human legifla-
" ture, it is religion ;" if they are bound by
no other rules than " the great principles of
" reafon and equity, and the general fenfe of
" mankind," and not by the more determined
principles of the Conftitution, nor fubject to
the controul of the People; if, by the influence
of corrupticn they are become " the Mafters,
" inftead of the Servants," of their Conftituents, looking *down* on the People, and *up* to
the Court for honours and preferments, and
granting money that they may receive it themfelves ; I fay, if thefe things be fo, and are they
not faid to be fc ? where is the difference betwixt a *free* and an *arbitrary* country ? where
the difference between the defpotifm of the
King of France, and the defpotifm of the Parliament of England ? And what is this but to
erect an *Ariftocratic* tyranny in the State, a
many-headed *Leviathan*, deplorable and to be
deplored, dangerous and deftructive, in propor-
tion to the numbers of which it confifts.

Hitherto I have confidered the *Supremacy* of
Parliament, or its *right to unlimited Power* in
and over *this Kingdom* ; and if I have fhewn,
that no fuch Power can exift in Parliament
from the very nature of its inftitution, for it is
a folecifm in politics, and an abfurdity in terms,
to fay, that in a *limited* Government, there can
be

be *unlimited* Power, the application of this Power over the Colonies muſt conſequently fall to the ground; and with it the occaſion of any further reaſoning upon the ſubject. But as Mr. Burke has made ſome aſſertions reſpecting this " unlimited legiſlative Power over the " Colonies," that are not only new and different from every other Writer, but new and different from himſelf too, I hope, I ſhall be excuſed the treſpaſs of a page or two more in the further conſideration of this matter.

Mr. Burke ſays, " When I firſt came into a " public truſt, I found your Parliament in poſ- " ſeſſion. of an *unlimited legiſlative Power* over " the Colonies. I could not open the Satute- " book without ſeeing the actual exerciſe of " it, more or leſs, *in all caſes whatſoever*." Theſe then are what I have called aſſertions without the ſhadow of proof, or more properly aſſertions with the moſt convincing proofs of their being without foundation ; for the proofs are taken from Mr. Burke himſelf. Here Mr. Burke ſays, " I could not open the Statute- " book without ſeeing the actual exerciſe of " this *unlimited Power* over the Colonies *in all* " *caſes whatſoever :*" but attend to what Mr. Burke ſays in his ſpeech on American Taxation, April the 19th, 1774, p. 40, 3d edit. printed for J. Dodſley, in. Pallmall. There he ſays, " This. is. *certainly* true ; that no Act avowed-
" ly

" ly for the purpofe of revenue, and with the
" ordinary title and recital taken together, is
" found in the *Statute-book* until the year
" 1764. All before this period ftood on *com-*
" *mercial* regulation and reftraint;" and to
prove this, that is, that a " Parliamentary in-
" land Taxation" was not to be found in the
Statute-book before the year 1764, is the bufinefs of this entire page: but as the extract
would be too tedious for this place, fo whilft I
refer the Reader to the page itfelf, I will take
the liberty of recommending to his perufal alfo
the whole Speech, as a moft excellent oration.
If then America was not " taxed *internally* for
" the purpofe of revenue before the year 1764,
" but all before this period ftood on *commer-*
" *cial* regulation," here is a cafe of Mr.
Burke's own former fliewing, that contradicts
the cafe he now puts, of an " actual exercife
" of unlimited legiflative authority over the
" Colonies *in all cafes whatfoever:*" for if Mr.
Burke could not find the exercife of this Power,
that is, of internal Taxation over the Colonies
for the purpofe of Revenue, in the *Statute-
book,* before the year 1764, no fuch Power
having been ever exercifed, he could not find
the exercife of *unlimited Power* over the Colonies *in all cafes whatfoever,* before the year
1764; and if he did not *then* find it, he could
not find it *after* the year 1764: for the firft
inftance of the exercife of this Power after
the

the year 1764, was that of the Stamp-Act;
and this Act, as foon as it paffed, was refifted,
and being refifted, it was repealed, and being
repealed, it could afford no proof of the poffeffion of the Power. And yet Mr. Burke
adds, " this poffeffion paffed with me for a
" title." But, if, as has been faid, Parliament
was not poffeffed of the Power of internal Taxation over the Colonies before the year 1764,
no title to unlimited legiflative Power *in all
cafes whatfoever*, before this time, could be
founded on poffeffion ; for here is a manifeft
exception to this poffeffion in the cafe of an
inland Taxation ; and from the year 1764, no
title can be derived from poffeffion, for the title
has been always difputed, and poffeffion never
obtained. So far then Mr. Burke is new and
different from himfelf. In what follows, he is
new and different from others.

No one has ever before contended, as I know
of, for the right of Parliament to tax America, without the annexed idea of America being reprefented in Parliament. The idle phan-
tom, the Cock-lane Ghoft, of *virtual* Reprefentation, has been ever conjured up, as the
ego fum ille, of this vile deception. But Mr.
Burke has afferted, has maintained, and has
proved, that America is not reprefented in Parliament, and yet infifts for the unlimited Right
in Parliament to bind America in all cafes

D   whatfoever.

whatfoever. He fays, " If any thing can be
" drawn from fuch examples by a parity of the
" cafe, it is to fhew, how deep their crime,
" and how heavy their punifhment will be,
" who fhall at any time dare to refift a diftant
" Power, actually difpofing of their property,
" *without their voice or confent to the difpofition*;
" and overturning their Franchifes without
" charge or hearing *."

Here then is his affertion, that America is
not reprefented in Parliament; and his affertion that Parliament has an *unlimited* legiflative
Power over America *in all cafes whatfoever*, has
been already ftated; which is a pofition as un-
accountable to me, as it is new. But let me
fee if fuch a pofition is defenfible, and whether
a queftion or two may not ferve as an anfwer
thereto. The firft queftion I fhall propofe is,
whether Reprefentation in order to Taxation
be not an *hereditary* indifpenfible privilege of
the Britifh Subject? The next queftion is,
whether the Americans are Britifh Subjects or
not? for if they are not Britifh Subjects, Great
Britain has nothing to do with them, no more
than France, or Spain, or any other country
has: And again, if they are Britifh Subjects,
and Reprefentation in order to Taxation is the
hereditary indifpenfible privilege of a Britifh
Subject, Reprefentation in order to Taxation

* See alfo Mr. Burke's Conciliatory Propofitions.

muft

muſt be the *hereditary* indiſpenſible privilege of
the Americans, as Britiſh Subjects. From whence
then can the Right to Parliament be derived of
unlimited legiſlative Power over the Subjects of
Great-Britain *in all caſes whatſoever* without
Repreſentation in Parliament, which the Americans do not poſſeſs, as Mr. Burke has ſhewn;
and which, in order to Taxation, is the *hereditary* indiſpenſible privilege of Britiſh Subjects? I preſume it cannot be derived from the
Conſtitution; for no man will aſſert, that the
Conſtitution gives a Right to Parliament to
levy Taxes upon Britiſh Subjects without Repreſentation; and if the Conſtitution does not
give this Right, the claim of it in Parliament
muſt be *unconſtitutional :* which naturally brings
me to the conſideration of the *declaratory Act*, as
falling under this point of view. Mr. Burke
has proved that America is not repreſented;
every wiſe man ſays the ſame; and it is only
folly the laſt that would aſſert the contrary.
The declaratory Act declares, and Mr. Burke
ſupports the declaration, that this country has
a right to bind America *in all caſes whatſoever;*
and of courſe to tax America, though not repreſented. Upon theſe principles is it poſſible
to maintain this Act? It has no foundation.
It reſts not upon the Conſtitution. It is ſubverſive of the Conſtitution. It has not the
fundamental requiſites of a declaratory Law.
No Law declaratory of Rights was ever before

made,

made, or ought to have been made, whose recital did not express the sources from whence
those Rights are derived; whether *direct* from
the Constitution, or *indirect* from other Acts
of Parliament founded on the Constitution, or
from general Customs, or particular Customs,
which make the Common Law of the Land.
Look from *Magna Charta*, through every declaratory Law, down to the *Act of Settlement*,
and it will be found that they are, every one
of them, *in perpetuum rei testimonium*, or testi-
monials only of what had *before* existed: But
this Law is declaratory not only of what never
existed *before*, but of a Right, against which
common usage, which is the *common Law of the
Land*, has been in direct opposition. I say in
direct opposition, for America, from beyond the
memory of man, nay, even from the very first
date of its civil existence to the era of this
reign, has been uninterruptedly used to the internal Taxation of itself.

This Law therefore must be repealed. As
it was enacted for the dignity of this country,
so for justice sake, which is the true dignity of
this country, let it now be repealed. It is
against Right, and usurped Power cannot up-
hold it. It is true the motives that brought it
into being were intentionally upright, but with
the patronage of the Author of those motives,
the motives themselves ceased; and of the Act
since,

fince, the *double Cabinet*, as Mr. Burke calls them, has made an infamous ufe. They knew not where to look for the Right of Taxation. They found it in this Act, and have fo tyrannized under it, that America has now ftamped its foot upon it, and will never ftir a ftep until " this tyranny be overpaft." Every ifland in the Weft-Indies look upon it with terror. All Ireland fee it with a jealous eye: For who is the Cafuift that can difcriminate between a Britifh parliamentary Right to tax America, and a Britifh parliamentary Right to tax Ireland? The cafe is the fame. The Right has been avowed in Parliament, and add to the 6. Geo. 1. ch. 5. or Irifh declaratory Act, the words only, " *in all cafes whatfoever*," and the matter is at iffue: but *Inexpediency* prevents the exercife. *Inexpediency!* curfe on the term! What may be *inexpedient* to-day, may be *expedient* to-morrow. *Inexpediency* is as the tyrant's fword, that hangs over the head, fufpended by a thread; and which *Difcretion* only is to keep from falling. But are Englifhmen to be thus *worded* out of their Rights? Forbid it, Common Senfe! Or rather let the fixed Principles of the Englifh Conftitution, and the eternal Rights of Humanity, be the fifter Fates to cut this Thread of Danger, by eftablifhing in its room — *Themfelves.*

One word more. It may be further afked,

D 3   What!

What! are the Americans to enjoy all the Rights appertaining to this Government, and not contribute to its support? I anfwer, by no means: it is not fitting they fhould. The fundamental Rights of the Englifh Conftitution I have fhewn to be, *the fecurity of Life, Liberty, Property, and Freedom in Trade*; and to thefe Rights all Britifh Subjects *within the realm*, are without exception, entitled, and fhould enjoy: but it is not fo with Britifh Subjects *out of the realm*, for *of them* fomething more is required, and *of them* fomething more has been received. They, (I mean the Colonifts) furrendered from the firft, one of the fundamental Rights of the Conftitution, to wit, *Freedom in Trade*. This they gave up, and this they put into the monopolizing hands of their brethren here, as the gift of Contribution, for the price of Protection. Excellent, and how valuable the exchange! when the very gift of contribution did itfelf enhance the price of protection! ineftimable jewel! than which a nobler did not grace the royal crown; and yet noble as it is, it was not enough to fatisfy the appetite of defpotifm. More muft be had. All was required. With *Freedom in Trade, Life, Liberty, and Property* were to be parted with; or, in the alternative, the revenge of *Herod* was to be taken in the blood of Innocents. Revenge has been purfued: but *Herod-like*, and I will ufe the language of the immortal Shakefpear;

When

When you fhall thefe unhappy deeds relate,
    then muft you fpeak,
Of one, whofe hand
Like the *bafe Judean* * threw a pearl away
Richer than all his Tribe.

I have now done with the Thoughts, which
the perufal of Mr. Burke's Letter had awaken-
ed in my mind; and find myfelf arrived at that
period where I had defigned to ftop : but as I
am upon the important fubject of America, as
there are one or two matters more that refting
on my mind, I could wifh to remove, and as I
fhall not again trouble the public with any further fentiments of mine upon this occafion (for
truth being my only object herein, I fhall as
readily look for it in others, as feek it in myfelf)
fo, if I fhould advance one or two paces beyond
my journey's end, I hope I fhall be excufed.

Having attended my duty in the Houfe of Lords
upon every important debate refpecting America,
it was there that I derived much ufeful information to myfelf : but yet, however inftructed, as I
truly have been, by the wifdom of thofe who
oppofed the meafure of a deftructive civil war,
I muft confefs, my mind has been more made
up on this fubject, by what has *not* been faid by
the advocates for it, than by what has been
advanced againft it. The *firft*, the *chief*, and

* This was Herod, who flew his Wife Mariamne.

      the

the *great champion* of all, for this calamity to a
country, has been the *now* Earl of Mansfield :
but his being fo, was to me, at the very firft
fight, an argument againft the war; for his
Lordfhip is no *warrior*, and therefore I fuppofed that if he had been more competent to
the events of fuch an undertaking, he had
been lefs *fanguine* in his recommendations of it,
Let us fee, however, what his arguments were.
The firft point to be fettled was, which of the
two countries was the *aggreffor*; and of courfe
which was to blame: but this would not bear
a difpute, for in the year 1764, when all was
peace and harmony between both countries,
this country, by its Stamp-Act, flung the firft
ftone at America, and fo (the year 1766 ex-
cepted) Great-Britain continued this *ftoning* of
America, like as Stephen was *ftoned*, to the
year 1775; when, by Negroes and Indians,
the Americans were to be *fcalped* and *flayed*
alive, even as Bartholomew was; and, in both
inftances, perhaps for the fame reafon: for
Stephen and Bartholomew were *Saints*, and the
Americans are called Diffenters, and Diffenters
are curfed, by fome Church-of-England-Men, as
Saints. To get rid then of this ftumbling-
block, of *aggrefforfhip*, fomething was to be
devifed; and this fomething was, that America
meant to become independent of this country :
But how was this to be fupported ? The learned
Lord proved it by *inuendoes*, by *fayings* and *do-*
ings,

ings, à priori, out of the American Affemblics; from Montcalm's Letters, which have been found to be forgeries; and from Kalm's Travels, who made a voyage to America in the year 1749, and who fays, that he was there told, that " the Englifh Colonies in North " America, in the fpace of thirty or fifty years, " would be able to form a ftate by themfelves, " independent of Old England." But here I muft beg leave to make an obfervation or two. Suppofing Mr. Kalm, inftead of going to North America in the year 1749, had come into England, and on his arrival had been told, that there were men in this country who *on their bare knees had drank the Pretender's health*; would not the inference have been juft as fair to fay, that this country meant to put the Pretender on the throne of this kingdom, in exclufion of the prefent family, as to fay, what Mr. Kalm does fay, that America meant independency ? I think it would : for the queftion is not what individuals fay, but what is the fenfe of the nation. And it is plain it was not the fenfe of this country to put the Pretender on the throne, and I hope it never will, notwithftanding his health has been fo drank, &c. &c. &c. &c. and what the fenfe of America was, appeared by the unanimous declaration of the people themfelves in the moft folemn and authentic manner. They fay, through their Congrefs, (and if ever the fenfe of any people

were

were taken, it was here found, for so free and general an election of Representatives was never before known in the annals of the world) " We " *chearfully* consent to the operation of such " Acts of the British Parliament, as are, *bona* " *fide*, restrained to the regulation of our ex- " ternal Commerce, for the purpose of securing " the commercial advantages of the whole em- " pire to the Mother Country," &c. &c. * It may be indeed said, that America has decla- red herself independent of this country, and therefore the prophecy of Mr. Kalm was true; but this does not follow: for this country, by putting America out of the protection of its laws, forced it, for self-preservation sake, into that state of Independency. Admitting, how- ever, that America did mean Independency, I will now ask, Were the measures pursued the means to prevent their becoming so? I appre- hend not: For although the force of this coun- try be sufficient for conquest, ten times its force would be insufficient to hold the country in sub- jection. Three millions of people, not only with their affections lost, but their inveterate hatred gained, at three thousand miles over the Atlantic, distant from the arm of power, are not so easily held prostrate at the feet of Parlia- ment, as Lord North was directed to say could be

* Vid. Votes of the Congress, reprinted for J. Almon, oppo- site Burlington-house, Piccadilly, and also the last Petition of the Congress to the King.

done

done. No: One hour of juftice and moderation would have done more, than all the German Blood-hounds hired from all the German Traffickers in Blood, in all the petty Principalities of Germany can atchieve in twenty years to come.

But to return to the learned Lord. Having fet up Independency, and upon what grounds I have fhewn, as the object of America; his Lorfhip argued, that the Rubicon was paffed, that we fhould kill the Americans, or the Americans would kill us, and that we could not look back, but muft go forward, though our deftruction be certain and inevitable. In fhort he drove us on, until we are all now driven, like fo many affes, into a *Found*; and are fo *impounded*, that Fourteen Shillings Land-Tax in the *Pound*, nay, all the *Pounds*, Shillings, and Pence in the Nation, will not *unpound* us. Such is our difgraceful, and truly to be lamented, fituation. The contempt of ourfelves, and the mockery of all Europe befides. Bullied by Frenchmen, infulted by Spaniards, memorialized by Dutchmen; and yet, happy would it be for us, if thefe were the only calamities that we are to fuffer.

Another argument for our entering into this favage War was, that the Americans were Cowards; an argument as full of indignity to this country, as it was of reproach to him that made it. Of Indignity, for are We to go to

war

war with our enemies becaufe they are cowards? Does Englifh valour want fuch motives of inducement for its exertion? Shameful reflection! Of reproach, for it was the argument of the firft Lord of the Admiralty, the Earl of Sandwich, that high Officer of the State, placed at the Head of the Britifh Navy. And is this the language of the gallant Navy of England? No: the brave love the brave, and had rather meet bravery in the wounds of themfelves, than cowardice in the difgrace of others. To fight with Cowards is the lofs of Honour, and " Honour is the Sailor's, as the Soldier's care." But the Americans are not Cowards, and this I fay for the honour of this country. If they were, fuch an Army and fuch a Navy doing no more than has been done in America, would well warrant the propriety of thofe incitements to action, which the Earl of Sandwich thought neceffary to hold out in the cowardice of America. When the Americans, therefore, are called Cowards by us, let us remember that it is not them, but ourfelves, that we accufe of Cowardice.

The laft argument I fhall take notice of, (for it is endlefs to recount the abfurdities that have been urged in fupport of this iniquitous warfare) and which I mention for that it feems to contain a fecret that fhould be known, is the argument of Lord Cardiff, fon of the Earl of Bute. His Lordfhip faid, as a reafon for carry-
ing

ing on this War of Parliament, that the Americans had offered to lay kingdoms at the feet of
the Crown, but which his Majesty disdained to
accept *. This is an heavy charge, and, as I
am as much an enemy to *arbitrary* power in
the Crown, as I am to *arbitrary* power in Parliament, if true, I must confess, except so far
as the justice of this nation is concerned in such
a war, I should feel little concern else for America: but as it seems very unnatural that men
should be surrendering their liberties, at the
very time that they are fighting for them, so I
have reason to believe that this argument has
been formed upon grounds that will not support
it. It is true, the Americans acknowledge the
authority of the King, and will not acknowledge
the authority of the Parliament. It is from
hence, therefore, I presume, inferred, that the
Americans are laying kingdoms at the feet of
his Majesty; and if so, to explain this matter,
is to remove the charge. The Americans were
the subjects of the Crown of England, and of
course owed allegiance to the King of England.
They were never the *subjects* of their *fellow-
subjects* the Parliament of England, and therefore neither owed nor professed allegiance to
Parliament. Besides, the King of England, by
the Constitution of England, cannot levy taxes
on his subjects; and therefore, for the Ameri-

* The Archbishop of York has adopted the same assertion.
See his Sermon, p. 22, and 23.

cans

cans to acknowledge the authority of the King, is no furrender of their property to the King: whereas if they acknowledged the authority of Parliament, who do exercife the right of taxation over the People when reprefented, it would be, without their being reprefented, a furrender of their property to Parliament; and a forging of chains for themfelves. Under the acknowledged authority, then of the Crown, the Americans ftill preferve their conftitutional Rights: under the *required* acknowledged authority of Parliament, they would lofe them; and this is the reafon that the Americans acknowledge the one, and will *never* acknowledge the other. But it is feared, that fome future King, not his prefent Majefty, for he has not a wifh to govern but through his Parliaments, may, upon requifition to his faithful American fubjects, procure fuch large grants of money, as fhall enable him to govern without Parliaments. Indeed, if we are to judge of what America may do, by what it has done, upon fuchlike occafions, this argument is not without its force; and therefore, to prevent fuch generofity from being hereafter hurtful to this country, (and there cannot be a better time for it, as it is the object of his prefent Majefty to maintain the *fupremacy* of Parliament,) let an Act be paffed, (if it be not too late) declaring that all money obtained from the Colonies by requifition from the Crown, fhall be carried

into

into the Exchequer, and accounted for in Parliament. This will remove the danger appre-
hended, and prevent thofe *lovers of flavery*,
the Americans, from making, at any future period, the Crown of England arbitrary.

Upon the whole, when I perceive a war, and
fuch a war too, fo weakly fupported, and yet
fo violently purfued; when I find the moſt
elevated of the Church, preaching and publiſh-
ing to the world paſſive obedience and non-re-
fiſtance to the fupremacy of Law *, whether
that Law be right or wrong, whether it be

---

* The Archbiſhop of York fays, " the foundation of legal freedom, is the *fupremacy of law*." This I fuppofe is an apology
for his Grace's *allegiance* to the Quebec-Act, and for his making this act a pattern for cramming Biſhopricks down the Throats
of the Americans, by the help of the Civil Power, that is, on the
points of Bayonets. See his Sermon, pag. 19 and pag. 24.

His Lordſhip fays too, " As there are in the nature of things,
" but two forts of Government; that of Law, and that of Force;
" it wants no argument to prove that under the laſt Freedom cannot
" fubfiſt." This is a diſtinction without a difference; for when
Law is contrary to the natural or civil rights of mankind, it
is *Force*, and the worſt of all *force:* for it is as " a wolf in
ſheep's cloathing," and cometh unawares, " like a thief in the
night. See p. 19 of the above fermon.

Again, his Lordſhip fays, " Thefe indeed" (that is " Def-
" potifm and Anarchy) have ufually *gone together*, for no Anar-
" chy ever prevailed, which did not *end* in Defpotifm." This
is a Bull, but an Iriſh one; and not a Popiſh Bull. If where
Anarchy prevails Defpotifm *ends*, Anarchy and Defpotifm cannot ufually *go together*. See p. 20.

His Grace will excufe the Attention I have paid him in the
courfe of my obfervations: but as I am unfortunately one of thofe
Parties who have (according to him) "no Principle belonging
" to them," and are " in the laſt ſtage of political Depravity,"
I was willing to examine, a little, his Lordſhip's principles;
that if I approved them, I might adopt them.

good or bad, whether it be to eftablifh Popery or Proteftantifm, whether it be enacted by an honeft, or by a corrupt and abandoned Parliament; when I fee men that were pillored in the reign of good old George II. penfioned in this, and for the fame reafons; when I hear of others hired to root out the very idea of *public virtue* from the minds, and tear *benevolence* from the hearts of Englifhmen; when I reflect, but why add more to the black catalogue of public dangers? It is time to look at home: it is time, even with *Stentorian* voice, to call for union among the Friends of the Conftitution: it is time that private opinion fhould yield to public fafety: it is time that we keep both " watch and ward," for if the liberties of our fellow-fubjects in America are to be taken from them, it is for the ideot only to fuppofe that we can preferve our own. The dagger uplifted againft the breaft of America, is meant for the heart of Old England. *Non agitur de vectigalibus, Libertas in dubio eft.*

In fine, thefe are my Sentiments, and thefe my Principles. They are the Principles of the Conftitution; and under this perfuafion whilft I have figned them with my Name, I will, if neceffary, as readily, feal them with my Blood.

F I N I S.

www.ingramcontent.com/pod-product-compliance
Lightning Source LLC
Chambersburg PA
CBHW021531090426
42739CB00007B/886